Table of Contents

Cricket: 500+ Amazing Facts from Around the World

1. Introduction: The Spirit of Cricket
2. Origins of the Game: Where It All Began
3. Historic Moments That Changed Cricket Forever
4. Legendary Players & Their Unbelievable Records
5. Fascinating World Cup Facts (Men & Women)
6. T20 Madness: Fastest Fifties, Hundreds & Wins
7. Unique Stadiums & Bizarre Ground Facts
8. Cricket in India: Passion Beyond Sport
9. Cricket in England: Birthplace of the Game
10. Australia: Dominance, Rivalries, & Records
11. Pakistan, Sri Lanka & Bangladesh: Subcontinent Surprises
12. South Africa & Zimbabwe: Resilience & History
13. New Zealand: The Gentle Giants
14. West Indies: Calypso Kings of Cricket
15. Afghanistan: The Meteoric Rise
16. USA, Ireland, Netherlands & Associate Nations
17. Funniest Moments in Cricket History
18. Controversies & Scandals: When Cricket Got Dark
19. Women in Cricket: Breaking Boundaries
20. Cricket and Technology: DRS, Hawk-Eye & More
21. Cricketing Nicknames & Their Backstories
22. Fastest Balls, Longest Sixes & Other Extremes
23. Rare Feats: Hat-tricks, Double Centuries & More
24. Cricket & Pop Culture: Movies, Songs & References
25. Conclusion: Why the World Loves Cricket

Introduction: The Spirit of Cricket

Cricket is not just a game — it's a feeling, a tradition, and a shared passion that connects billions across the globe. Whether it's the roar of the crowd at Lord's in England, the electrifying energy in Mumbai's Wankhede Stadium, or the rising enthusiasm in emerging nations like the USA and Nepal, cricket has become much more than a sport. It is a cultural phenomenon.

The spirit of cricket lies in **respect** — respect for the game, the opponents, the officials, and the fans. From the earliest days when the sport was played by English aristocrats in the 16th century to modern-day stadiums packed with fans waving colorful flags and chanting for their heroes, cricket has evolved without losing its essence.

One of the unique aspects of cricket is its **gentleman's code of conduct.** Even in the heat of competition, sportsmanship often shines through — players applauding opponents' performances, offering help when someone is injured, or walking off even before the umpire gives a decision. While emotions run high, the soul of cricket encourages fairness and honor.

What makes cricket so special is its **variety of formats** — Test matches that stretch over five days, One-Day Internationals (ODIs) that mix patience with aggression, and T20s that are fast-paced entertainment spectacles. Each format brings a different flavor but carries the same heartbeat: strategy, skill, and excitement.

Cricket is also a game of **stories and legends**. From Sir Donald Bradman's unmatched batting average to MS Dhoni's cool finishing moves, from the fierce Ashes rivalry to the IPL's glitz and glamor — cricket is a goldmine of unforgettable moments. The beauty of the game lies in its unpredictability — a single over can change the fate of an entire match, a tail-ender can become a hero, or a young debutant can overshadow legends.

Over time, cricket has broken barriers of race, class, and gender. Women's cricket is rising rapidly, drawing crowds and creating new role models. Technology like DRS, UltraEdge, and Hawk-Eye have made the game fairer and more thrilling for viewers worldwide. Cricket has even crossed into pop culture — films, songs, advertisements, and even fashion trends reflect its influence.

Above all, cricket binds communities. In India, it is often described as a religion. In Australia, it's a summer ritual. In the Caribbean, it's a celebration. And in new territories like the USA, Germany, and Canada, cricket is finding new homes and fresh voices. No matter where it's played — on dusty village grounds or world-class arenas — cricket speaks a universal language.

This book is a tribute to that spirit — filled with 500 fascinating facts that will entertain, surprise, and deepen your love for the game. Whether you're a hardcore fan, a curious learner, or someone who grew up listening to cricket commentary with your family, welcome aboard.

Let's journey through the rich world of cricket, one amazing fact at a time.

Chapter 2: Origins of the Game – Where It All Began

The story of cricket is as rich and fascinating as the game itself. Long before giant stadiums, colored jerseys, and millions of fans cheering on television, cricket began as a **simple pastime in the English countryside.** Its origins can be traced back over **800 years** — to a time when even the concept of professional sports didn't exist.

The earliest known reference to cricket comes from **southern England in the 13th century**, where it was believed to be played by children using a stick and a ball made of wool or stone. Back then, cricket wasn't played on lush green pitches — it was played on meadows, with **sheep grazing nearby and trees acting as wickets.**

By the **17th century**, cricket had become a popular game among adults, especially in rural villages. Matches were often informal but competitive, with local pride on the line. Slowly, it spread across counties, and **gambling became a common part of cricket matches.** Wealthy landowners and noblemen began organizing matches and backing teams, which laid the foundation for cricket as a spectator sport.

The **first official cricket club**, the **Hambledon Club**, was established in the 1760s in Hampshire, England. But the real transformation came in **1787**, when the **Marylebone Cricket Club (MCC)** was founded at **Lord's** in London. The MCC became the guardian of cricket laws and played a crucial role in shaping the rules of the modern game — from bat size and pitch length to scoring and player conduct.

During the **British Empire's expansion**, cricket traveled beyond England's borders. Soldiers, traders, and missionaries carried the game with them to **India, Australia, South Africa, the Caribbean, and beyond.** What began as a colonial sport was soon embraced passionately by the people of these nations. In fact, countries like India and the West Indies didn't just adopt cricket — they made it their own, creating unique styles, rivalries, and legends.

The first **international cricket match** was played in **1844 between the USA and Canada**, not England! But it was in **1877** that the first official **Test match** took place — between **Australia and England** in Melbourne. This match marked the beginning of international cricket as we know it today.

Cricket also reflected the **social and political changes** of the time. In India, the sport became a way for locals to challenge their colonial rulers. In the Caribbean, cricket gave the oppressed a platform to rise and shine. The game became a symbol of unity, pride, and resistance — far more than just sport.

As we journey through this book, you'll see how this game — born in English villages — grew to become a global obsession. From village greens to urban stadiums, from wooden bats to high-tech gear, from handwritten scores to big-screen replays — cricket's origin story is a beautiful blend of tradition, struggle, and evolution.

Cricket's roots may be old, but its spirit is forever young.

Chapter 3: Historic Moments That Changed Cricket Forever

Cricket isn't just made of matches — it's made of *moments*. Moments that echo in stadiums long after the game ends. Moments that leave fans teary-eyed, breathless, or leaping with joy. Some moments define a player's career, others define the sport itself. Let's take a time-travel through some of the most iconic moments that truly changed the face of cricket forever.

1. 1983 – India's World Cup Miracle at Lord's

No one expected India to win. The mighty West Indies were two-time world champions, and India were the underdogs. But on **25th June 1983**, under the captaincy of **Kapil Dev**, India stunned the world by winning the **Cricket World Cup** at Lord's. Kapil's iconic 175* against Zimbabwe earlier in the tournament is still considered one of the greatest one-man efforts in cricket. This win changed Indian cricket forever — it transformed cricket from just a sport to a religion.

2. 2005 – The Greatest Ashes Ever

England vs Australia — the fiercest rivalry in cricket. But the **2005 Ashes series** took that rivalry to legendary heights. From Andrew Flintoff's all-round brilliance to nail-biting finishes, this series had it all. England won the Ashes after **18 years**, and the streets of London flooded with fans. It reignited global interest in Test cricket and reminded the world that the long format still had magic.

3. 2007 – T20 World Cup & the Dhoni Era Begins

Cricket changed forever in 2007 when the first **T20 World Cup** was held. It was fast, flashy, and full of drama. India, under a young and fearless

MS Dhoni, lifted the trophy after a nail-biting final against Pakistan. The match ended with **Joginder Sharma bowling the final over**, and the celebration was wild. This win laid the foundation for the **IPL**, which began in 2008, and turned T20 into a global craze.

4. 2010 – Sachin Tendulkar's Double Century in ODIs

It took almost 40 years of ODI cricket for someone to score a double hundred. And it had to be **Sachin Tendulkar** — the 'God of Cricket'. On 24th February 2010, in Gwalior, he scored *200 against South Africa**, setting a new benchmark. The world stood still. News channels flashed the headline for hours. It wasn't just a record — it was a reward for decades of dedication.

5. 2019 – The World Cup Final That No One Can Forget

England vs New Zealand — **World Cup 2019 final** — one of the most dramatic matches in sports history. Scores were tied. Super Over followed. And even that ended in a tie. England won on **boundary count rule** — a method that was debated worldwide. But what no one debated was that it was the **most intense, emotional, and unbelievable cricket final ever played.** It showed how thrilling cricket could be, even in its most technical moments.

6. 2006 – South Africa Chase 434!

When Australia posted **434/4 in 50 overs**, no one imagined it could be chased. But South Africa did the unthinkable. **Herschelle Gibbs smashed 175**, and in the final over, SA reached 438. It was the highest chase in ODI history and one of the most entertaining matches ever played. Fans watching around the world couldn't believe what they had just witnessed.

These were not just moments — they were emotions carved in time. They inspired millions to pick up a bat, wear a jersey, or cheer till their throats hurt. These moments made cricket the *heart* of many nations.

And the best part? **The next historic moment might happen tomorrow.** That's the magic of cricket.

Chapter 4: Legendary Players & Their Unbelievable Records

Cricket, like every great sport, has been shaped by extraordinary individuals — players whose talent, passion, and consistency have etched their names into history. These legends have not just played the game; they have *defined* it. Their records are more than numbers — they are milestones that narrate stories of greatness, perseverance, and legacy.

Let's journey through some of the most iconic figures in cricket and their awe-inspiring achievements.

---

1. Sachin Tendulkar – The Master Blaster (India)

No discussion of cricket legends can begin without mentioning **Sachin Tendulkar**. Regarded as the greatest batsman of all time, he carried the hopes of a billion people every time he stepped on the pitch. Over a 24-year career, he amassed records that remain untouched.

Unbelievable Record:

- *100 international centuries* — the only player in history to achieve this feat.
- Most runs in both Tests and ODIs.
- First cricketer to score a double century in ODIs.

His presence united nations, and his humility made him a global icon.

2. Muttiah Muralitharan – The Spin Wizard (Sri Lanka)

When it comes to bowling dominance, **Muttiah Muralitharan** stands alone at the top. With his magical spin, uncanny variations, and unmatched control, he baffled even the greatest batsmen.

Unbelievable Record:

- *800 wickets in Test cricket* — the highest ever by any bowler.
- *1,347 international wickets* in all formats — a towering record.

His legacy continues to inspire spinners across the globe.

3. MS Dhoni – The Ice-Cool Finisher (India)

Cool under pressure, sharp behind the stumps, and lethal with the bat — **MS Dhoni** was a captain like no other. From small-town beginnings to global stardom, his leadership redefined Indian cricket.

Unbelievable Record:

- The *only captain in history* to win all three major ICC trophies:
    - T20 World Cup (2007)
    - ODI World Cup (2011)
    - Champions Trophy (2013)

Dhoni's unmatched calmness and finishing ability made him one of the most respected players worldwide.

4. Brian Lara – The Caribbean Genius (West Indies)

Known for his elegance and explosive shot-making, **Brian Lara** was an artist with the bat. Watching him play was like witnessing a masterpiece in motion.

Unbelievable Record:

- *Highest individual score in Test cricket*: 400* not out.
- The only player to reclaim the Test record after losing it — showing sheer dominance.

Lara's flair brought style and swagger to cricket.

---

5. Virat Kohli – The Modern Maestro (India)

Intensity, fitness, and consistency define **Virat Kohli**. A modern-day great, Kohli has been the face of Indian cricket in the 2010s and 2020s. His hunger for runs and passion for the game is unmatched.

Unbelievable Record:

- *Fastest to 8,000 to 13,000 ODI runs*.
- *50 ODI centuries* — surpassing even Sachin Tendulkar's legendary 49.
- Over 25,000 runs in international cricket before turning 35.

Kohli has become a role model for athletes worldwide.

---

6. AB de Villiers – Mr. 360 (South Africa)

A true entertainer, **AB de Villiers** changed how cricket was played. With the ability to hit shots all around the ground — from traditional cover drives to unorthodox scoops — he earned the nickname "Mr. 360."

Unbelievable Record:

- *Fastest ODI century*: just 31 balls.
- Multiple records for fastest 50s and 150s in ODIs.

His creativity and sportsmanship made him one of the most loved cricketers on the planet.

7. Ellyse Perry – The Queen of Modern Women's Cricket (Australia)

Cricket is not just a men's game — and **Ellyse Perry** is proof. Representing Australia in both cricket and football, she's one of the greatest female all-rounders of all time.

Unbelievable Record:

- Represented Australia in both *FIFA Women's World Cup* and *Cricket World Cup*.
- Scored a double century in Tests and took hundreds of international wickets.

She has been a game-changer for women's sports globally.

These legends have turned cricket into an emotion, a spectacle, and a legacy. Their records are not just achievements — they are *chapters in cricket history*, studied, celebrated, and remembered by generations.

And who knows — the next legend might be practicing in a backyard right now.

Chapter 5: Fascinating World Cup Facts (Men & Women)

When it comes to cricket, no tournament captures the spirit, rivalry, drama, and glory quite like the **Cricket World Cup**. Whether it's the men's mega-events or the rising dominance of the women's game, every World Cup writes history in gold.

Here are some fascinating, jaw-dropping facts that make the Cricket World Cup the ultimate sporting spectacle.

Men's Cricket World Cup Facts

1. The First Men's World Cup (1975)
The inaugural tournament was hosted by **England**. It was a 60-over format, played in white kits with red balls — a far cry from today's colorful one-dayers.

2. India's 1983 Miracle Win
India stunned the cricketing world by beating the dominant West Indies in the final. Kapil Dev's 175* vs Zimbabwe in that tournament is still considered one of the greatest ODI innings.

3. Australia's World Cup Domination
Australia has won the tournament **6 times** (1987, 1999, 2003, 2007, 2015, 2023) — the most by any team. Their dominance between 1999 and 2007, winning 3 in a row, is unmatched.

4. Fastest Century in a World Cup
Ireland's **Kevin O'Brien** scored a century off just **50 balls** against England in 2011 — the fastest in WC history at the time, leading to a historic upset.

5. Highest Team Total
South Africa smashed **428/5** against Sri Lanka in the 2023 World Cup — the highest team total in WC history.

6. Most Runs in a Single Tournament
India's **Sachin Tendulkar** scored **673 runs** in the 2003 World Cup — a record that stood until **Virat Kohli** broke it in 2023 with **765 runs**.

7. Most Wickets in a Single Tournament
Australia's **Mitchell Starc** (2019) and Sri Lanka's **Chaminda Vaas** (2003) both took **26 wickets**, with Starc doing it in fewer matches.

8. World Cup Hat-tricks
Chetan Sharma (1987) was the first to take a WC hat-trick. Lasith Malinga (2007, 2011, 2019) remains the only player to have multiple hat-tricks across tournaments.

9. First Super Over World Cup Final
The 2019 final between England and New Zealand ended in a tie — twice! After the Super Over, England won on boundary count. It was the most dramatic finish in cricket history.

10. The All-Rounder Magic
Yuvraj Singh in 2011: 362 runs, 15 wickets, 4 MoM awards, and the Player of the Tournament. He did it all — while battling cancer.

Women's Cricket World Cup Facts

1. The First Women's World Cup (1973)
Held **two years before** the men's, the first WWC was won by **England**. This was a revolutionary step for women's cricket.

2. Australia's Record Reign
Australia's women's team has won **7 World Cups** (1978, 1982, 1988, 1997, 2005, 2013, 2022) — the most in women's history. They are the queens of cricket dominance.

3. Highest Individual Score
Belinda Clark of Australia scored *229 off 155 balls** vs Denmark in 1997 — the first ever double century in ODI history, male or female.

4. India's Rise (2005 & 2017)
India reached the finals twice. In 2017, *Harmanpreet Kaur's 171 vs Australia** became an iconic moment in women's cricket, showcasing power, flair, and fearlessness.

5. Most Wickets in Women's World Cups
Lyn Fullston (Australia) holds the record with **39 wickets** across tournaments — a record that stood for decades.

6. Fastest Fifty in Women's WC
New Zealand's **Sophie Devine** smashed a fifty off just **18 balls** — one of the fastest in the women's game.

7. Meg Lanning: A Captain's Story
Leading from the front, Australia's Meg Lanning won multiple titles and is one of the most successful women's cricket captains ever.

8. Most Runs in a Single Women's WC
Debbie Hockley (New Zealand) scored **456 runs** in the 1997 World Cup — a stunning display of consistency.

9. Emerging Stars
The 2022 Women's World Cup introduced future stars like **Shafali Verma**, **Smriti Mandhana**, and **Alyssa Healy**, who are now global names.

10. Global Reach & Broadcast Growth
The 2017 final between India and England drew over **180 million viewers** — a historic moment that boosted women's cricket visibility worldwide.

Fun World Cup Trivia

- Only two teams have won both men's and women's World Cups: **Australia** and **England**.
- India has hosted or co-hosted the **men's World Cup four times** — more than any other country.
- **Ricky Ponting** remains the only captain to win two back-to-back men's World Cups (2003 & 2007).

Conclusion:

From trailblazing women in the 1970s to nail-biting Super Overs in 2019, the Cricket World Cup — in both its forms — has constantly evolved, amazed, and inspired. These fascinating facts remind us that cricket isn't just a game; it's a powerful story of passion, unity, and pride.

Chapter 6: T20 Madness – Fastest Fifties, Hundreds & Wins

If cricket had an adrenaline mode, it would be **T20** — the shortest, wildest, and most thrilling format of the game. It's fast-paced, power-packed, and perfect for those who love instant action. In just 3 hours, T20s deliver sixes, upsets, drama, and madness like no other format.

Let's dive into the fastest fifties, jaw-dropping hundreds, and lightning-quick victories that define the chaotic beauty of T20 cricket.

Fastest Fifties – When Batsmen Went Berserk

In T20s, you don't settle. You **smash from ball one.**

1. Yuvraj Singh – 12 Balls of Pure Destruction (2007)
 During the 2007 T20 World Cup, Yuvraj Singh turned into a human fireball. After a spat with Andrew Flintoff, he unleashed pure rage on Stuart Broad, hitting **six sixes in an over** and reaching a **50 in just 12 balls** — a world record that still stands.

2. Chris Gayle – 12-Ball Mayhem in IPL (2013)
 Though Yuvraj holds the international record, Gayle matched the madness in the IPL. His 12-ball fifty for Royal Challengers Bangalore showed what true power-hitting looks like.

3. KL Rahul – 14-Ball Blitz
 Rahul's 14-ball fifty vs Delhi in the IPL reminded everyone that timing + class = carnage.

Other Notables:

- Marcus Stoinis – 17 balls
- Moeen Ali – 16 balls
- Glenn Maxwell – 18 balls (and a lot of reverse sweeps!)

Fastest Hundreds – Storms in Human Form

When a batter hits a hundred in under 40 balls, you're not watching cricket — you're watching fireworks.

1. David Miller – 35 Balls of "Killer Miller" (2017)
South Africa's David Miller annihilated Bangladesh with a **35-ball century**, saying, *"If it's in the arc, it's out of the park."*

2. Rohit Sharma – 35-Ball Elegance (2017)
Rohit, known for his lazy elegance, showed brutal force against Sri Lanka, tying Miller's record. His innings was a mix of timing, power, and calm.

3. Sudesh Wickramasekara – 35 Balls (Czech Republic)
Yes, Czech Republic! The growth of cricket is real. This knock proved that T20s are giving lesser-known teams a moment in the spotlight.

4. Chris Gayle – 30-Ball IPL Hundred (2013)
Let's be real — this was **the** most iconic T20 knock ever. Gayle scored *175 in 66 balls**, with **17 sixes**. Opponents didn't bowl; they survived.

Quickest Team Wins – Blink and It's Over

Sometimes teams don't just win — they **humiliate**.

1. Sri Lanka vs Netherlands (2014)
Sri Lanka bowled out the Dutch for **39 runs** and chased the target in **just 5 overs**. It was like watching a lion hunt a rabbit.

2. India vs Scotland (2021 T20 WC)
India skittled out Scotland for 85, then chased it in **6.3 overs** — a savage reminder of their power when the top order fires.

3. Australia vs Sri Lanka (2007)
Bowled them out for **87**, then chased the target in **10.2 overs**. It was so clinical, it looked scripted.

Honorable Mentions – Pure Madness

- **Hazratullah Zazai (Afghanistan)** hit **6 sixes in an over** in a T20 match and made 162* off 62 balls.
- **Aaron Finch** once scored **172 runs in a T20I**, the highest ever in international T20s.
- **Lasith Malinga** took **4 wickets in 4 balls** in a T20I. Yorkers with surgical precision.
- **India vs Bangladesh (2016)** — Bangladesh needed 2 runs in 3 balls… and still lost. Nail-biting drama!

Conclusion: The Beauty of T20 Chaos

T20 cricket is a rollercoaster of madness — no time to blink, no time to breathe. It's the format where **heroes are born in 20 balls**, and **legends are made in 120 deliveries**. Whether it's a 12-ball fifty or a game won in under an hour, T20 is where cricket breaks its own rules — and we absolutely love it.

Chapter 7: Unique Stadiums & Bizarre Ground Facts

Cricket is not just about the players and the action — it's also about the **arenas** where legends are born and history is made. Stadiums, with their quirks, grandeur, and at times, outright *bizarre features*, add a unique flavor to the game. From snow-covered pitches to grounds built on rooftops, cricket has truly traveled to some **unbelievable places**.

Let's take a global tour of the **strangest**, **highest**, **largest**, and most **jaw-dropping cricket stadiums** and the mind-blowing facts that come with them.

1. The Floating Cricket Pitch – Maldives

Yes, you read that right. The Maldives built a **floating cricket pitch** on water, mainly to promote tourism. Imagine hitting a six and watching the ball disappear into the endless ocean!

- No stands, no crowd — just blue sky and blue water.
- Played for exhibition matches and high-profile photo shoots.

This is what you call "cricket on waves!"

2. The World's Highest Cricket Ground – Chail, India

At **7,500 feet above sea level**, Chail Cricket Ground in Himachal Pradesh is a slice of heaven surrounded by deodar trees.

- Built in **1893** by the Maharaja of Patiala.
- Not used for international matches but remains a **record holder**.
- The air is so thin that the ball travels *faster and further*.

A match here feels like cricket among the clouds.

3. The Stadium with a Tree Inside – St. Lawrence Ground, Canterbury (UK)

There used to be a **massive lime tree inside the playing field**! Yes, fielders and bowlers had to **work around the tree**.

- If the ball hit the tree, it wasn't a six.
- The tree became so iconic that it was left standing for over a century.
- Sadly, it was brought down by a storm in 2005 — but its legacy lives on.

It's probably the only time a *tree was part of the fielding unit!*

---

4. The World's Largest Stadium – Narendra Modi Stadium, India

Located in Ahmedabad, this **monumental stadium** can hold a mind-blowing **132,000 spectators** — the **largest cricket stadium on Earth**.

- Spread across 63 acres with four dressing rooms and LED-lit seating.
- Hosted major IPL and World Cup matches.
- Watching a match here feels like witnessing a **cricket carnival**.

The roar of the crowd here is not noise — it's *thunder*.

---

5. The Most Unusual Shape – Eden Park, New Zealand

Eden Park isn't round or oval — it's kind of… *squarish*. This makes hitting sixes both easier and riskier, depending on which side you're playing.

- The **straight boundaries are super short**.
- Bowlers fear it, batters love it.
- The angles confuse even the best fielders.

It's like playing cricket in a cricket-shaped box!

6. The Pitch on Ice – Switzerland

Cricket on **ice**? Welcome to the annual **Ice Cricket Challenge** held in St. Moritz, Switzerland.

- Players wear winter gear and spike shoes.
- The pitch is carved out on a frozen lake.
- Legends like Sehwag and Afridi have played here.

Where else do you get to hit a six with snow falling around you?

7. Sahara Stadium – Changing Names Like Jerseys

The stadium in Durban, South Africa, is known for **changing names constantly** — from Kingsmead to Sahara Stadium to Hollywoodbets Kingsmead.

- A running joke among fans who can't keep up.
- Still one of the **fastest pitches** in the world.
- Famous for wild bounce and even wilder rain interruptions.

No one's quite sure what it'll be called next season!

8. Pitch With a Slope – Lord's Cricket Ground, England

You'd think the pitch would be flat, right? Not at **Lord's**, the "Home of Cricket."

- The pitch has a **slope of 2.5 meters** from one end to the other.
- Fast bowlers love bowling downhill.
- It messes with the minds of even the best batters.

Only in England could a slope become a strategy.

9. Stadium with a Swimming Pool – Gabba, Australia

The **Gabba** in Brisbane comes with a **swimming pool and BBQ zone** inside the stadium!

- Yes, you can chill in the pool while watching a match.
- It's like a backyard party — but with international cricket going on.
- Ideal place for a summer match and a cold drink.

Now *that's* how you make cricket truly cool.

10. The Ground That's Technically Not in a Country – Pitch in the No-Man's Land

Believe it or not, there was once a pitch built on a border area — with one half in **Belgium** and the other in **the Netherlands**.

- Players could technically run between countries during a match!
- While not an official stadium, it was used for friendly cricket games.
- No visa needed to play here — just a passion for the game.

Conclusion: Beyond the Boundary

Cricket stadiums aren't just places — they're **characters in the story**. Some are majestic, others mysterious, and a few downright mad. But each one adds flavor, history, and unpredictability to the beautiful game. From trees in the outfield to floating pitches, cricket reminds us that the field of play can be as wild and wonderful as the sport itself.

So the next time you watch a game, don't just admire the players — look around. You might just spot something **bizarre, beautiful, or both.**

Chapter 8: Cricket in India – Passion Beyond Sport

In India, **cricket is not just a game**—it's a **religion**, a **festival**, a **national obsession**, and for many, a **way of life**. From bustling cities to quiet villages, dusty playgrounds to glittering stadiums, cricket echoes through every street, every screen, and every heart.

To say that India *loves* cricket would be an understatement. India **lives** it, **breathes** it, and **dreams** it.

From Gully to Glory: Where Dreams Begin

For most Indians, cricket starts not in academies, but in the **gullies**—narrow streets where anything can be a bat, and a pile of bricks serves as stumps. Tennis balls fly over parked cars, neighbors yell at kids for broken windows, and every six hit into someone's balcony is a mini World Cup victory.

- These street matches are where champions are born.
- Players like **MS Dhoni**, **Jasprit Bumrah**, and **Hardik Pandya** rose from humble beginnings.

Every kid in India has, at some point, imagined themselves as the next **Kohli** or **Sachin** while smashing a six over a boundary made of schoolbags.

Heroes in Blue: The National Obsession

When Team India plays, **time stops**. Offices empty, roads go silent, and eyes lock onto TV screens. Whether it's a World Cup final or a Test match in England, **1.4 billion hearts** beat as one.

- A six from Rohit Sharma lights up homes like Diwali.
- A wicket from Bumrah feels like justice served.
- A victory? It's a national celebration.

There are **temples with Sachin's photos, stadiums named after cricketers**, and **babies named Virat**. That's not fandom—it's *faith*.

The IPL Revolution: Cricket Meets Bollywood

The launch of the **Indian Premier League (IPL)** in 2008 changed everything. Suddenly, cricket became a **mega spectacle**—a thrilling mix of sport, glamour, and drama.

- Teams owned by Bollywood stars and billionaires.
- Cheerleaders, fireworks, theme songs.
- Players from India, Australia, South Africa, and even Afghanistan playing side by side.

IPL isn't just cricket—it's **entertainment on steroids**. And for many fans, it's the **highlight of the year**.

Cricket as a Social Connector

In India, cricket breaks barriers.

- It brings together Hindus and Muslims, rich and poor, north and south.
- Strangers become friends when they cheer for the same team.
- Entire families bond over evening matches, shouting at the TV like the players can hear them.

From wedding halls with live cricket screenings to college fests centered around match days—**cricket unites India like nothing else can.**

The Pressure and the Glory

With passion comes pressure. Indian cricketers don't just play for victory—they play for the expectations of a billion fans.

- One missed catch can invite nationwide criticism.
- One century can turn a player into a living legend.

But despite the pressure, Indian players rise. Because they know they carry not just bats and balls—but **the hopes of a nation**.

Beyond the Game

Cricket has transformed Indian culture, media, fashion, and even language. Words like "googly," "doosra," and "sixer" have become part of everyday talk.

- Sports shops thrive selling replica jerseys.
- Kids wear helmets and gloves before they wear school ties.
- Movies, ads, and memes are filled with cricket references.

From brand endorsements to blockbuster biopics like *MS Dhoni: The Untold Story*, cricket is everywhere.

Conclusion: India's Eternal Love Affair

Cricket in India is more than a sport—it's a story. A story of hope, struggle, unity, and triumph. It's the tale of a country that finds joy in every cover drive, every hat-trick, and every nail-biting finish.

As long as the sun shines on dusty grounds and echoes of "Sachin! Sachin!" ring through the air, India's love for cricket will never fade. Because here, **cricket is not played. It is worshipped**.

Chapter 9: Cricket in England – Birthplace of the Game

If cricket were a grand old novel, then **England is the first page**—the origin, the cradle, the storyteller. It's here that the game was **born on village greens**, whispered through ancient pubs, and slowly evolved into the sport that would one day unite billions.

England gave the world more than tea and the English language—it gave us **cricket**.

From Sheep Fields to Lords

Cricket's earliest whispers trace back to the **13th century**, when shepherds in southeast England supposedly played a bat-and-ball game on grassy meadows. What began as a rural pastime for farmers soon caught the attention of the aristocracy, and by the **18th century**, it was being played in proper matches with crowds and stakes.

Then came **Lord's Cricket Ground** in 1814—often called "The Home of Cricket." With its iconic pavilion and the quirky slope on the pitch, it remains a symbol of the game's rich history and elegance.

The Gentlemen's Game

In England, cricket grew with a sense of **etiquette and tradition**. The sport wasn't just about runs and wickets—it was about **grace, sportsmanship, and character**.

- Players wore white.
- Games were paused for tea.
- Umpire's decisions were final—even if debatable.

This aura of sophistication led to cricket being dubbed the **"Gentlemen's Game"**—a label that still lingers, even as modern cricket becomes more explosive and commercial.

The Ashes: A Fierce Rivalry is Born

In 1882, something extraordinary happened: **Australia beat England at The Oval**, and a mock obituary appeared in the papers declaring, "The body of English cricket will be cremated and the ashes taken to Australia."

Thus, **The Ashes** were born—**cricket's oldest and fiercest rivalry**.

Since then, England and Australia have fought timeless battles, producing:

- Unforgettable moments (like Ben Stokes' miracle at Headingley),
- Legends (like Sir Ian Botham, Alastair Cook, and Andrew Flintoff),
- And emotions that shake stadiums and living rooms alike.

England's Modern Cricketing Soul

While England was steeped in Test match tradition, it faced criticism for being **too slow to adapt** to shorter formats. That changed with a bang.

In 2019, under the leadership of **Eoin Morgan**, England transformed into an **aggressive, fearless white-ball team**—culminating in one of the greatest finals in cricket history.

- **2019 World Cup Final** at Lord's vs New Zealand.
- Super Over. Tied scores. England win by boundary count.
- The world was in awe. **England were world champions.**

It was the **perfect storm of tradition meeting modern flair.**

The County System: Nurturing Talent

England's strength also lies in its **County Cricket** structure. With 18 counties competing in formats from T20 to first-class cricket, it's a powerful training ground for nurturing future stars.

Names like **Joe Root, Jofra Archer, and Harry Brook** have risen through this system—sharp, skilled, and ready to wear the Three Lions on their chest.

The Fans, The Fields, The Feeling

From the grassy hills of The Oval to the beer-fueled roars of Edgbaston, English cricket fans are among the most passionate and witty in the world. They sing, sledge, and celebrate with both elegance and edge.

- The **Barmy Army** travels the world backing England with drums and chants.
- **Village cricket** continues on sunny weekends—picnics, pints, and playful sledging.
- Even rainy days are part of the experience—after all, it's England!

Conclusion: The Keeper of Tradition

England may not dominate cricket as it once did, but it still holds something more powerful—**legacy**. It's the guardian of cricket's traditions, the keeper of its oldest rivalries, and the place where the game still wears a tie and raises a toast after a match.

In England, cricket isn't just a sport—it's a living, evolving piece of cultural identity. And while the game has travelled far and wide, it always remembers where it came from.

Because in the heart of England, **cricket was not just invented—it was immortalized**.

Chapter 10: Australia – Dominance, Rivalries & Records

When you think of cricketing powerhouses, **Australia stands tall—bold, fierce, and unstoppable**. The Aussies didn't just play cricket—they **rewrote the rules of dominance**, forged legendary rivalries, and left behind a trail of world records that still dazzle fans across generations.

For Australia, cricket isn't just about winning. It's about **intimidating, innovating, and inspiring**.

The Aussie Spirit: Grit, Aggression & Glory

From sun-baked schoolyards in Sydney to massive stadiums in Melbourne, Australians grow up with a cricket bat in hand and a winning mindset in their heart.

They're known for:

- **Fearless batting**, brutal fast bowling, and mental toughness.
- Sledging that pushes boundaries—and opponents.
- A never-say-die attitude that makes every match a battle.

Whether it's a World Cup final or a street game on Christmas, Aussies play hard, play smart, and play to **win**.

Golden Eras & Living Legends

Australia has enjoyed multiple golden generations, each packed with **icons who defined the game**:

- **Sir Donald Bradman** – the greatest batsman of all time, with an unmatched Test average of **99.94**.
- **Shane Warne** – the magician who made the ball dance and revived leg spin.
- **Ricky Ponting** – captain courageous and one of the finest batsmen in history.
- **Glenn McGrath, Adam Gilchrist, Steve Waugh, Michael Clarke** – the list goes on.

No country has produced such a **lethal combination of flair and fear**.

World Cup Kings

If cricket had royalty, **Australia would wear the crown**.

- 5 ICC Cricket World Cup titles (1987, 1999, 2003, 2007, 2015)
- The only team to **win three World Cups in a row**
- Reached **7 World Cup finals**—more than any other nation

Their dominance in the early 2000s was **frightening**. Teams would fear the green and gold jersey, knowing defeat often felt inevitable.

The Ashes: More Than Just a Series

Perhaps the most iconic rivalry in cricket history is the **Ashes battle between Australia and England**.

This is **not just a series—it's a war of pride, history, and national honor**.

From the fiery exchanges of the Bodyline series to modern-day classics:

- Australia has produced unforgettable Ashes heroes like **Steve Smith**, **Mitchell Johnson**, and **Justin Langer**.
- Every win on English soil is celebrated like a festival back home.

For Aussies, **beating England in the Ashes is like winning a war**—and they never take it lightly.

Unforgettable Moments & Records

Australian cricket is filled with **jaw-dropping records** and **goosebump moments**:

- **Matthew Hayden's 380** vs Zimbabwe in 2003—then the highest Test score.
- **Brett Lee's 160+ km/h missiles**—terrorizing batters worldwide.
- *Michael Clarke's 329 in Sydney*, pure batting beauty.
- **2007 World Cup final**: Gilchrist's explosive 149 that crushed Sri Lanka.

Their record books are not just long—they're legendary.

The Baggy Green: A Symbol of Honor

In Australia, receiving the **Baggy Green cap** is sacred. It's more than a uniform—it's a badge of national pride, resilience, and legacy.

- Every player treasures it.
- Every fan respects it.
- And every performance under it adds to the legend.

As Steve Waugh once said, *"The Baggy Green is not just a piece of cloth. It's a symbol of everything Australian cricket stands for."*

Modern-Day Titans

Today's generation—led by stars like **Pat Cummins, Steve Smith, Marnus Labuschagne, Travis Head, and Mitchell Starc**—continues the legacy of domination.

In **2021–23**, Australia won the **World Test Championship**, retained the **Ashes**, and lifted the **2023 ODI World Cup**—beating India in India, no less.

The message? **Australia is never done winning**.

Conclusion: The Relentless Roar of Aussie Cricket

Australia isn't just a cricket team. It's a **machine**. A cricketing culture that blends talent, toughness, and tradition into something almost unbeatable.

They don't just play to entertain—they play to **dominate**, to **humble** their rivals, and to keep their place at the top.

Whether it's under the scorching sun of Perth or the packed stands of the MCG, Australian cricket always brings **drama, discipline, and destruction**.

And that's why, for many, **Australia is the beating heart of world cricket**.

Chapter 11: Pakistan, Sri Lanka & Bangladesh – Subcontinent Surprises

Cricket in the Indian subcontinent is more than a sport—it's a **religion, a festival, and a battle of emotions**. While India often takes the spotlight, its neighbors—**Pakistan, Sri Lanka, and Bangladesh**—have delivered some of the most unforgettable moments in cricketing history. These nations have thrilled the world with their **flair, unpredictability, passion, and heroic underdog stories.**

Let's explore how each of these teams carved their own unforgettable path into cricketing glory.

Pakistan: Unpredictable, Untamed & Unforgettable

If there's one team in world cricket that's impossible to predict, it's **Pakistan**. One day, they lose to an associate nation. The next, they blow away the world champions. That's the beauty—and the madness—of Pakistani cricket.

- **Raw pace?** Pakistan had it first—with the likes of **Wasim Akram, Waqar Younis**, and **Shoaib Akhtar**, the fastest bowler ever.
- **Mystery spin?** Think **Saqlain Mushtaq** and **Abdul Qadir**.
- **Street-fighter batting?** From **Javed Miandad** to **Shahid Afridi**, Pakistanis never back down.

They are the **masters of chaos**—but also of brilliance.

Major Highlights:

- **1992 World Cup Champions** – Under the leadership of charismatic **Imran Khan**, Pakistan roared from the brink of elimination to ultimate glory.
- **2009 T20 World Cup Champions** – A comeback story powered by flair, aggression, and team unity.
- **Champions Trophy 2017** – They stunned India in the final, a victory that still echoes in Pakistani streets.

Their unpredictability is their weapon. When Pakistan plays, expect **fireworks and drama**.

Sri Lanka: The Island of Innovation & Heart

Cricket on the tropical island of **Sri Lanka** is a source of national pride and unity. The islanders bring a **graceful, intelligent, and unorthodox flair** to the game.

- **Sanath Jayasuriya** revolutionized power-hitting in ODIs.
- **Muttiah Muralitharan** spun a web around the cricketing world with **800 Test wickets**—a record that may never be broken.
- **Kumar Sangakkara** and **Mahela Jayawardene** are the epitome of elegance and class.

From being underdogs to world champions, Sri Lanka's journey is nothing short of magical.

Major Highlights:

- **1996 World Cup Champions** – Led by Arjuna Ranatunga, the team rewrote history by defeating the giants and lifting the trophy.
- **2014 T20 World Cup Champions** – A tribute to the golden generation as Sangakkara and Jayawardene bowed out in style.
- **Consistent Finalists** – They reached the finals of three consecutive ICC tournaments from 2007 to 2011.

Sri Lanka proves that **you don't need a massive population to be cricketing giants—you need heart, strategy, and unity.**

Bangladesh: The Rising Tigers

Bangladesh may have been the newest member of the Test cricket family in the 21st century, but they've evolved at a stunning pace. What began as a team struggling to win a match turned into one of the **most passionate and feared sides**, especially in home conditions.

- Their **fanbase is electrifying**—stadiums in Dhaka and Chattogram erupt like volcanoes.
- Players like **Shakib Al Hasan**, **Tamim Iqbal**, **Mushfiqur Rahim**, and **Mashrafe Mortaza** became household names across the world.

Major Highlights:

- **2007 & 2015 World Cups** – Shocked the world by beating giants like India, South Africa, and England.
- **2017 Champions Trophy** – Reached the semi-finals, marking their arrival on the big stage.
- **Asia Cup Finalists** – They've pushed India and Pakistan to the edge on multiple occasions.

Bangladesh is no longer the "minnow" of cricket—they are **hungry, aggressive, and determined to dominate.**

The Subcontinental Magic

What ties these three countries together is their **passion, unpredictability, and love for the game**. You'll find:

- Kids playing cricket with bricks and sticks in back alleys.
- Millions glued to the TV during every match.
- Tears of joy and heartbreak for every win and loss.

And even though their journeys are different, **Pakistan, Sri Lanka, and Bangladesh have one thing in common**—they play with soul. Their cricket is emotional, volatile, and unforgettable.

Conclusion: Heroes, Heartbreaks & Hope

While the world often expects dominance from India or Australia, these subcontinental nations have constantly reminded everyone: **cricket is a game of surprises.**

- Pakistan is the **wild artist**, painting magic on the field with speed and drama.
- Sri Lanka is the **wise craftsman**, blending strategy and elegance.

- Bangladesh is the **roaring tiger**, still rising, still fighting, and always dreaming.

Together, they keep the spirit of subcontinental cricket **vibrant, thrilling, and gloriously unpredictable.**

Chapter 12: South Africa & Zimbabwe – Resilience & History

In the grand theatre of world cricket, the tales of **South Africa** and **Zimbabwe** are not just about trophies or records—they're stories of **resilience, redemption, struggle, and silent brilliance**. These two nations from the heart of Africa have given the cricketing world **legendary players**, unforgettable matches, and a reminder that **spirit often outshines silverware**.

South Africa: The Uncrowned Kings

No team in cricket history has combined **talent, heartbreak, and perseverance** quite like **South Africa**. Nicknamed the **Proteas**, they were banned from international cricket for over two decades due to apartheid and only returned in 1991. Since then, they've produced some of the **greatest cricketers the game has ever seen**.

Legends of the Game:

- **Jacques Kallis** – One of the most complete all-rounders in cricket history.
- **AB de Villiers** – Mr. 360. The man who made the impossible look effortless.
- **Dale Steyn** – A pace machine with unmatched aggression and control.

- **Hashim Amla, Graeme Smith, Mark Boucher, Allan Donald** – Each a giant in his own right.

Major Highlights:

- **Consistent World Cup Semifinalists** – 1992, 1999, 2007, and 2015 saw South Africa come agonizingly close but fall just short.
- **Test Supremacy** – For a time, they were the No.1 ranked Test team, defeating top nations home and away.
- **2023 ODI World Cup** – Showed flashes of dominance, continuing their reputation as a powerhouse.

But for all their brilliance, the Proteas are often remembered for their **heartbreaking exits**—from the rain-rule fiasco in 1992 to the tied semi-final in 1999. The world calls it the **"chokers" tag**, but real cricket lovers know better—**they're warriors** who've fought fate as fiercely as any team.

Zimbabwe: Grit Against the Odds

If South Africa's story is one of brilliance and near misses, **Zimbabwe's** tale is of **survival, courage, and flashes of brilliance amidst chaos**.

Political turmoil, lack of infrastructure, and player exodus didn't stop Zimbabwe from producing **moments of magic**.

Cricketing Gems:

- **Andy Flower & Grant Flower** – Elegant, dependable, and often the lone warriors in tough times.
- **Heath Streak** – A lion-hearted fast bowler who gave everything for his country.
- **Tatenda Taibu** – The youngest ever Test captain at 20 and a symbol of Zimbabwean resilience.
- **Brendan Taylor** – A modern-day warrior with a bat in hand and steel in his heart.

Major Moments:

- **1999 World Cup** – Shocked South Africa and India, reaching the Super Six stage.
- **2003 World Cup** – Progressed to the Super Six again, giving bigger teams a run for their money.
- **Upsets Galore** – From defeating Australia in 1983 to Pakistan in 2022, Zimbabwe has made every big team sweat.

Cricket in Zimbabwe survives because of **passion**, not politics. Fans cheer in empty stadiums, and players train with limited gear—but **the heart never fades**.

Shared Legacy: Strength in Struggle

What binds **South Africa and Zimbabwe** is not just geography, but a shared cricketing DNA of **fighting against adversity**.

- South Africa's players have carried the weight of expectations, and despite not having a World Cup, they've earned the respect of the world.
- Zimbabwe's cricketers have played not for fame or fortune, but for **pride and love for the game.**

In a world obsessed with wins and trophies, these nations teach us something deeper—**that true greatness lies in resilience, in passion that doesn't fade with loss, and in playing with purpose.**

Conclusion: African Spirit, Global Impact

Whether it's a Dale Steyn yorker tearing through stumps or Andy Flower playing a lone masterclass, the cricketing world owes **Africa a chapter in its golden book**.

South Africa remains a **sleeping giant**, always threatening to rise and conquer.

Zimbabwe remains a **symbol of stubborn hope**, refusing to disappear.

And together, they remind us: **Cricket is more than just statistics—it's about soul.**

Chapter 13: New Zealand – The Gentle Giants

In a world where cricket often roars with fierce rivalries and loud aggression, **New Zealand** walks in softly—with humility, grace, and quiet confidence—yet leaves a thunderous impact. Nicknamed the **Black Caps**, New Zealand is the epitome of the phrase **"let your game do the talking."** They may not always dominate headlines, but they have won the hearts of millions with their sportsmanship, fighting spirit, and unshakable team bond.

Cricketing with Class

New Zealand's cricketers are known not just for their talent but for being **true gentlemen of the game.** Whether it's offering a hand to a fallen opponent or smiling through heartbreaking losses, they play the game **the way it was meant to be played—fairly and fiercely.**

Their success story is not one of overnight stardom but **slow, steady, and silent growth**—from being underdogs to becoming one of the most consistent sides in all formats.

Legends of the Land of the Long White Cloud

- **Kane Williamson** – Calm, composed, and arguably one of the most technically gifted batsmen in the world. A captain who leads with his brain and heart.

- **Brendon McCullum** – The man who brought aggression and flair to New Zealand cricket. His 2015 World Cup leadership changed it all.
- **Martin Crowe** – A visionary batsman from the past whose style still inspires.
- **Daniel Vettori** – One of the finest left-arm spinners and a true cricketing brain.
- **Ross Taylor, Tim Southee, Trent Boult, Stephen Fleming** – All legends who built the Black Caps' legacy.

Moments That Defined Their Legacy

- **2015 Cricket World Cup**: Co-hosts and finalists. McCullum's fearless leadership and the last-ball thriller against South Africa in the semi-final became the stuff of legends.

- **2019 Cricket World Cup**: The most **heartbreaking yet honorable loss** in cricket history. After tying the final and the Super Over against England, New Zealand lost on a boundary count—a rule so controversial that it was abolished later. But their grace in defeat earned global respect.

- **WTC 2021 Final**: Redemption. In the inaugural **World Test Championship**, New Zealand outclassed India in the final, proving that they were not just nice guys—they were **world champions**.

What Makes Them Special?

- **Team Over Individuals**: You won't find over-the-top egos or flashy celebrations here. Every Black Cap plays for the team. Success is shared, and blame is carried together.

- **Adaptability**: From swinging pitches in Wellington to flat decks in Dubai, New Zealand adapts to conditions better than most.

- **Unbreakable Unity**: Whether it's a young debutant or a senior legend, every player is treated with respect. Their dressing room is known to be one of the most peaceful and balanced in world cricket.

Cricket Meets Kiwi Culture

New Zealand's cricket reflects its culture—**respectful, nature-loving, and fiercely loyal.** The love for the game runs deep in the small population of just over 5 million. From backyard cricket with friends to packed stadiums in Auckland and Christchurch, cricket here is more than a sport—**it's a symbol of pride.**

The Black Caps are loved not only at home but across the world. Ask any neutral fan, and chances are, **they'll root for New Zealand.**

Conclusion: Humility is Power

They may not have the largest fan base, the flashiest players, or the richest board, but New Zealand has something far more powerful—**character.**

They are the **gentle giants** of world cricket. Polite in speech, brutal with the ball. Humble in interviews, lethal in performances. They've shown the world that you don't have to shout to be heard.

In a game often filled with noise, New Zealand whispers greatness—and the world listens.

Chapter 14: West Indies – Calypso Kings of Cricket

There was a time when the mere mention of **West Indies** sent a chill down the spine of the best batting line-ups in the world. From the sun-kissed beaches of the Caribbean came a team that didn't just play cricket — **they danced with it, destroyed with it, and defined swagger** long before the word became cool. They weren't just champions; they were **cricketing royalty draped in maroon**, ruling the world with charm and carnage.

The Rise of the Kings

The West Indies' golden era began in the 1970s and roared through the 1980s. This wasn't a team; it was a **storm in white flannels**. Fast bowlers who spat fire. Batsmen who batted like poetry in motion. And an attitude that said, "We play hard, we play fair, and we win with flair."

Key Moments:

- **1975 & 1979** – Won the first two Cricket World Cups with style and domination.
- **Unbeaten Test Series** – For over 15 years, they were virtually unbeatable in Test cricket.
- **World T20 Champions** – Winners in **2012** and **2016**, proving their legacy was far from over.

The Legends Who Ruled the Game

West Indies cricket has produced some of the **most iconic names** in the sport — legends whose names still echo in stadiums around the world.

- **Sir Vivian Richards** – The master of swagger, fearless, explosive, and always in control.

- **Brian Lara** – The prince of Port of Spain, holding the record for *highest individual Test score (400)**.
- **Clive Lloyd** – The powerful leader who captained the golden generation.
- **Malcolm Marshall, Michael Holding, Joel Garner, Andy Roberts** – The **four horsemen of fast bowling**, destroying batsmen with pace and precision.
- **Chris Gayle** – The self-proclaimed Universe Boss, redefining T20 batting with brutal sixes.
- **Dwayne Bravo, Andre Russell, Sunil Narine, Kieron Pollard** – The T20 superstars of the modern game.

Calypso Style – More Than Just a Game

What set the West Indies apart wasn't just their skill — it was their **style**. Cricket for them was joy, rhythm, and celebration. Their approach was soaked in **calypso beats**, and every boundary felt like a carnival. Even during the toughest battles, their **smiles and swag never left the field**.

They played cricket like it was meant to be played — **with heart, humor, and honor.**

Challenges & The Road Ahead

In recent decades, the West Indies have struggled with consistency. Internal politics, lack of infrastructure, and player conflicts have dimmed the glow of their once-dominant crown. But even in their lows, **they continue to produce match-winners**.

Their **2024 T20 World Cup campaign**, hosted on their own shores, showed glimmers of revival — a team rebuilding with young blood and fearless energy.

Legacy That Lives On

The West Indies may not dominate like they once did, but their **impact on cricket is immortal**. They brought soul, spirit, and spectacle to the game. From the towering sixes to toe-crushing yorkers, from Bob Marley vibes to packed Caribbean stadiums — **they gave cricket its coolest chapter.**

Conclusion: Royalty in Rhythm

The West Indies taught the world that cricket could be **art**, **war**, and **celebration** all in one. They are not just a team; they're a **culture**, a **movement**, a **heartbeat of cricket's soul**.

They may not always win, but when the maroon army takes the field, one thing's for sure — **cricket becomes magic again.**

Chapter 15: Afghanistan – The Meteoric Rise

In a world where cricketing giants have ruled for over a century, the rise of **Afghanistan** is nothing short of a modern-day fairytale. From dusty streets and war-torn landscapes to roaring stadiums and global headlines, the Afghan cricket team has emerged as a symbol of **hope, resilience, and unstoppable ambition**.

This isn't just a cricket story — it's a **miracle wrapped in a dream**, written by warriors who turned adversity into artistry.

From Refugee Camps to Cricket Fields

The seeds of Afghan cricket were sown in the refugee camps of **Pakistan** during the Soviet-Afghan war. Young boys, displaced from their homeland, picked up the bat and ball to escape reality — and unknowingly, started a revolution. What began as a coping mechanism became a national obsession.

By **2001**, Afghanistan had a national cricket team. By **2017**, they had achieved **Test status**, joining the elite club of cricket nations. The speed of this rise was almost **unimaginable** — like watching a comet blaze through the sky.

Heroes of the Afghan Revolution

Afghanistan's rise has been fueled by a group of fearless cricketers who made the world take notice.

- **Mohammad Nabi** – The heart and soul of Afghan cricket. A true all-rounder, a calm leader, and a global T20 star.
- **Rashid Khan** – A teenage prodigy who became a global sensation. With his deadly leg-spin and cool composure, Rashid has become **Afghanistan's biggest cricketing export**.
- **Mujeeb Ur Rahman** – A mystery spinner who made his debut at just 16 and has puzzled world-class batsmen with ease.
- **Najeebullah Zadran, Rahmanullah Gurbaz, Fazalhaq Farooqi** – Young guns who've brought firepower, flair, and fearlessness.

These players are not just athletes — they are **national icons**.

Cricket Amidst Chaos

What makes Afghanistan's journey even more inspiring is the backdrop — a country struggling with political instability, conflict, and uncertainty. But cricket has united the people like nothing else. It has become **a language of hope** in a land where despair often dominates the headlines.

Every Afghan victory is more than just a win — it's **a moment of national pride**, a rare breath of joy in difficult times.

T20 Titans & World Cup Warriors

Afghanistan has especially thrived in the T20 format. Their performances in World Cups and Asia Cups have **rattled giants and thrilled fans**.

- In the **2021 T20 World Cup**, they dominated group stages with powerful wins and competitive flair.
- In **ODI formats**, they've defeated teams like **Sri Lanka, Bangladesh, and even Pakistan**, proving they are no pushovers.
- Their **2023 and 2024 World Cup campaigns** showed maturity, talent, and serious intent.

They're no longer the underdogs. They're **contenders**.

The Spirit of the Team

What sets Afghanistan apart is their **fearless approach**. They don't play with pressure — they play with **purpose**. Their bowlers are lethal, their batsmen aggressive, and their fielders charged with raw energy. Every game they play feels like a war cry.

Looking Ahead: The Future is Bright

With a young and hungry core, Afghanistan's future in cricket looks blazing. With investments in domestic leagues, infrastructure, and youth development, the team is only going to **get stronger**.

The dream? To one day lift a World Cup trophy — and at this pace, it no longer feels impossible.

Conclusion: The Phoenix That Rose

Afghanistan's cricket story is a testament to the human spirit. From rubble to recognition, they've defied every odd and silenced every critic. They didn't just rise — **they soared**, faster and fiercer than anyone expected.

In the grand narrative of cricket, Afghanistan has carved a chapter that will be remembered for generations — the story of **The Meteoric Rise**.

Chapter 16: USA, Ireland, Netherlands & Associate Nations – Cricket's Expanding Frontier

In the grand halls of cricketing history, names like India, Australia, and England echo loudest. But beyond the traditional powerhouses, a new wave of passion, talent, and ambition is rising. Countries once seen as outsiders are now writing their own chapters in the cricketing saga. From the skyscrapers of **USA** to the green fields of **Ireland**, the picturesque stadiums of the **Netherlands**, and the dreams of countless **Associate Nations** — cricket is going global like never before.

USA: The Sleeping Giant Awakens

When people think of sports in the United States, they think of **NBA, NFL, MLB** — but **cricket**? Not yet. But that's changing — fast.

With a large South Asian, Caribbean, and British expat community, the **cricket craze in the U.S.** is growing rapidly. The launch of **Major League Cricket (MLC)** in 2023 was a game-changer. With international stars, world-class venues, and significant investments, MLC brought top-tier cricket to American soil.

- **USA National Team** has also made headlines, especially with their qualification for **ICC tournaments** and victories over full-member nations.
- Players like **Ali Khan** have gained recognition through leagues like the **CPL** and **IPL**.

As cricket eyes the **2028 LA Olympics**, the USA could very well become the sport's next big market.

Ireland: The Giant Killers

Ireland has been one of cricket's most exciting underdog stories. They burst into the global spotlight in the **2007 Cricket World Cup**, defeating **Pakistan** and shocking the world. But they didn't stop there.

- In 2011, they pulled off one of the most famous chases in World Cup history by defeating **England**, thanks to **Kevin O'Brien's** unforgettable century.
- Ireland became a **Test-playing nation in 2017**, solidifying their place among cricket's elite.
- They've consistently produced gritty, fearless cricketers — from **William Porterfield** to **Paul Stirling**, **Andrew Balbirnie**, and **Josh Little**.

Ireland may be small in size, but their cricketing heart is massive.

Netherlands: The Orange Warriors

The Dutch are no strangers to cricket. The Netherlands has participated in multiple World Cups and stunned cricket fans with their fearless brand of play.

- Who could forget their dramatic win against **England in the 2009 T20 World Cup** at Lord's?
- Or their **2023 World Cup campaign**, where they defeated **South Africa** and **Bangladesh**, proving they're not here just to participate — they're here to compete.

Players like **Bas de Leede**, **Logan van Beek**, and **Scott Edwards** have become global names. The Dutch team represents the perfect mix of **European flair and cricketing fire**.

Associate Nations: Cricket's Growing Army

Beyond these three, there's a long list of Associate Nations — **Scotland, Nepal, Namibia, UAE, Oman, Papua New Guinea**, and more — all building strong cricketing cultures.

- **Nepal**, with its breathtaking mountains and cricket-mad youth, packs stadiums like few others.
- **Namibia** impressed the world in T20 World Cups with their fighting spirit.
- **Scotland** has repeatedly punched above its weight, defeating teams like **England** and **Bangladesh**.
- **UAE and Oman** have hosted major ICC tournaments and built cricketing infrastructure that rivals full-member nations.

These countries may not have the financial muscle or historic legacy of the big boys, but they bring **raw hunger, pride, and promise**.

The Road Ahead: More Than Just Expansion

The inclusion of these nations isn't just about numbers — it's about **globalizing cricket**. The ICC's new formats, funding models, and efforts to take the game to new regions have opened doors for exciting talent and untapped markets.

In the coming years, expect more upsets, more unforgettable moments, and perhaps, **new World Cup contenders** from the unlikeliest of places.

Conclusion: Cricket Without Borders

Cricket's soul lies in competition, culture, and community — and these emerging nations are bringing fresh colors to the canvas. With booming fan bases, rising stars, and dreams larger than life, the USA, Ireland, Netherlands, and other Associate Nations are not just expanding cricket's map — they're **reshaping its future**.

The game is no longer confined. **Cricket is everywhere. And everyone's invited.**

Chapter 17: Funniest Moments in Cricket History – When the Gentleman's Game Got Hilariously Wild

Cricket is often called the "gentleman's game" — a sport of rules, respect, and regal competition. But every now and then, this elegant sport delivers moments of sheer hilarity that leave fans, commentators, and even players in splits. From accidental bloopers to witty banter, cricket has had its fair share of rib-tickling episodes. Let's dive into the lighter side of cricket — **the funniest moments in cricket history**.

1. The "Hit-Wicket" While Celebrating

Imagine this: You hit a six, raise your bat in celebration — and get out! That's exactly what happened when India's **Ravi Jadeja**, during a domestic match, smashed a six, twirled his bat flamboyantly… and accidentally knocked over the stumps with his foot. Hit-wicket dismissal, crowd stunned, memes born.

2. Inzamam-ul-Haq's Epic Run Outs

Legendary Pakistani batsman **Inzamam-ul-Haq** was known for his powerful batting — and comically slow running. Inzy's run-outs were a category of comedy on their own. One time, he tripped, got up, ran again, and still got out — all in slow motion. The umpire was laughing. So were the fans.

3. Steve Waugh's Invisible Ball

During a Test match, **Steve Waugh** was batting when a ball hit the stumps, bails flew off, and the bowler celebrated. But replays showed something hilarious — **the ball missed the stumps completely!** It was the wind that blew the bails off, but the bowler thought he got a wicket. Oops!

4. The "Dance-Off" Run-Up

In a Caribbean Premier League match, **Kesrick Williams** celebrated wickets by writing names in his imaginary notebook. Enter **Virat Kohli** — who smashed him for boundaries and then mimicked his celebration. Fans loved the banter. Williams laughed later too — but not that day!

5. Andrew Flintoff's "Airplane" Celebration

After dismissing Tino Best, England's **Andrew Flintoff** stretched his arms and ran across the pitch like an airplane. Tino had tried to hit a six and got out instead. It was cheeky, silly, and absolutely unforgettable.

6. When Batsmen Forgot to Run

In a match between **Sri Lanka and India**, the batsman hit the ball and stared at it... but forgot to run. The non-striker screamed, "Run, run!" but both just stood there. The fielders were confused too. Result? Run out — and a thousand facepalms.

7. Dhoni's No-Look Run Out

In true "cool" style, **MS Dhoni** once pulled off a no-look run-out. The ball came in, Dhoni didn't even glance at the stumps — just flicked his wrist, and *boom* — direct hit, batter out. Everyone was shocked. Dhoni didn't even blink.

8. Shahid Afridi's "Missing the Ball" Dance

Pakistani power-hitter **Shahid Afridi** once tried to slog a spinner so hard, he missed it completely, spun 360 degrees like a ballerina, lost his helmet, and nearly fell over. The bowler couldn't stop laughing. Neither could the crowd.

9. The "Helmet" Six

During an IPL match, **Rishabh Pant** played a shot that went straight up in the air. The ball came down and *landed on his own helmet*, which had fallen to the ground. It bounced off and went to the boundary. Four runs. Everyone confused. Rulebook said... runs count!

10. Duck for Dinner

In an ODI, a literal duck (the bird) wandered onto the pitch. The game had to stop. Players tried to gently chase it away. The crowd chanted, "Duck! Duck!" Hilarious coincidence? The next batter was dismissed for a duck too. That's some next-level symbolism!

Conclusion: A Game Full of Laughs

Cricket isn't always serious. In between intense battles and heroic performances, there are moments of pure joy, unpredictability, and laughter. These funny incidents are what make the sport **so human, so relatable, and so unforgettable**.

Because sometimes... cricket is just *too funny* to handle!

Chapter 18: Controversies & Scandals – When Cricket Got Dark

Cricket is a sport that unites nations, inspires billions, and builds legends. But behind the cheering crowds and glorious centuries lies a darker side — a world where fame, money, and pressure sometimes lead to scandals, controversies, and decisions that shake the game's very soul. From match-fixing and ball-tampering to ugly on-field fights, cricket has had its share of shame. This chapter dives deep into the moments when cricket wasn't so "gentlemanly."

1. The Match-Fixing Storm of 2000

The biggest black mark in cricket history came at the turn of the millennium. South African captain **Hansie Cronje**, respected worldwide, shocked the cricket world when he admitted to accepting money from bookmakers to fix matches. The scandal shook fans to their core. Cronje was banned for life, and suddenly, the game's purity was under serious doubt. This led to massive reforms — but the damage was done.

2. Pakistan's Spot-Fixing Scandal (2010)

In 2010, during a Test match at Lord's, Pakistani bowlers **Mohammad Amir**, **Mohammad Asif**, and captain **Salman Butt** were caught in a sting operation accepting money to bowl deliberate no-balls. The nation wept, fans were heartbroken, and all three players were banned and even jailed. The incident reminded the world: even rising stars can fall hard.

3. The "Sandpapergate" Scandal (2018)

Australia, known for its tough cricketing culture, faced international shame when **Cameron Bancroft** was caught on camera using sandpaper to tamper with the ball during a Test in South Africa. Skipper **Steve Smith** and vice-captain **David Warner** were implicated and banned for a year. Cricket Australia was rocked, and the image of Australian cricket took a severe hit. Smith's teary press conference is etched in fans' memories.

4. The Monkeygate Incident

During India's tour of Australia in 2008, a heated exchange between **Harbhajan Singh** and **Andrew Symonds** turned into an international controversy. Symonds alleged racial abuse, claiming Harbhajan called him a "monkey." The incident created tension between the two teams and almost caused India to pull out of the tour. Though charges were later dropped, it exposed cultural friction in international cricket.

5. The IPL Brawls & Drama

While the Indian Premier League brought glamour to cricket, it also brought chaos. Players fought on-field (remember **Gambhir vs. Kohli**?), owners got into trouble, and franchises were banned due to betting and fixing charges. **Chennai Super Kings** and **Rajasthan Royals** were suspended for two years after team officials were found guilty of illegal betting. The league survived, but the cracks were visible.

---

6. Umpire Bias & DRS Drama

Cricket controversies aren't just about players. Umpires have often been at the center of storms. Accusations of bias, especially during crucial matches, have led to outrage. The **2008 Sydney Test** between India and Australia was full of controversial decisions — sparking massive criticism of umpires and eventually leading to the wider adoption of DRS (Decision Review System).

---

7. Political Tensions on the Pitch

Cricket has often become a battleground for political tensions — especially between **India and Pakistan**. Matches have been canceled, players banned, and fans divided due to political interference. At times, governments have stepped in to block tours or World Cup matches. In such cases, cricket becomes more than a game — it becomes a symbol of international relations.

---

8. Racial Discrimination in the Game

Racism in cricket has existed silently for decades. From the apartheid-era ban on South Africa to recent accusations of racist abuse by English county players, the issue has been deep-rooted. In 2020, the **Black Lives Matter** movement sparked a global conversation in cricket too. Players like **Michael Holding** delivered emotional speeches, calling for lasting change.

Conclusion: Shadows Behind the Spotlight

Cricket is a beautiful game, but it's not immune to human flaws. These scandals and controversies remind us that heroes can fall, systems can fail, and even the cleanest sport can get dirty. But they also show the sport's ability to rise again, rebuild trust, and move forward stronger.

Because at the end of the day, while darkness may visit, the **spirit of cricket always fights back**.

Chapter 19: Women in Cricket – Breaking Boundaries

For decades, cricket was seen as a "gentleman's game." But the ladies had other plans. With sheer determination, unmatched skill, and unshakable passion, **women in cricket** have shattered stereotypes, broken boundaries, and carved out a place that's not just equal—but extraordinary.

From dusty local grounds to the grandest World Cup stages, women cricketers have redefined what it means to wear the jersey. This chapter is a tribute to their journey, their fight, their glory.

1. The Unsung Beginnings

Women's cricket didn't start yesterday. In fact, the first recorded women's cricket match was played in **1745** in England. But recognition came much later. The **Women's Cricket Association** was formed in 1926 in the UK, followed by the **International Women's Cricket Council (IWCC)** in 1958.

The journey was slow, with little funding, barely any coverage, and minimal crowd support. Players often bought their own kits and paid for travel just to represent their countries. But they never stopped playing. They played for the love of the game.

2. Game-Changing Moments

The first Women's Cricket World Cup took place in **1973**—two years before the men's! England won it, and suddenly, the world took notice. But it wasn't until the **2017 ICC Women's World Cup**, hosted in England, that women's cricket truly exploded. Over **180 million viewers** watched the final. Social media lit up. Stadiums were packed.

India vs England at Lord's was more than a match—it was a movement. Players like **Mithali Raj**, **Harmanpreet Kaur**, and **Smriti Mandhana** became household names in India. In Australia, stars like **Ellyse Perry** and **Meg Lanning** inspired an entire generation.

3. Records that Dazzle

Women's cricket is not just about passion—it's about power, skill, and stunning records.

- **Belinda Clark** of Australia scored the first-ever double century in an ODI—*229 runs**—way back in 1997.
- **Jhulan Goswami**, India's pace queen, is the highest wicket-taker in Women's ODIs.
- **Alyssa Healy's** blazing century in the 2020 T20 World Cup Final at the MCG was watched by **86,000 fans live**—a world record for a women's sporting event in Australia.

These feats are not just "good for women's cricket"—they're legendary by any standard.

4. T20 Revolution & Global Leagues

The T20 format has transformed women's cricket. It brought in flash, firepower, and a global audience. The **Women's Big Bash League (WBBL)** in Australia and **The Hundred** in England have become powerhouses of talent. India followed suit with the **Women's Premier League (WPL)**, launched in 2023, featuring fierce international competition and record-breaking auctions.

Finally, women cricketers are earning the spotlight, salaries, and respect they deserve.

5. More Than Just Cricketers

These women are more than athletes. They're role models, pioneers, and changemakers. **Mithali Raj** fought gender bias to lead India for over two decades. **Shabnim Ismail** from South Africa overcame a tough upbringing to become one of the fastest bowlers in the world. **Nida Dar**, **Deepti Sharma**, **Amelia Kerr**—each name tells a story of courage, culture, and confidence.

6. The Road Ahead

Women's cricket is still growing. Yes, there's still a gap in pay, sponsorship, and visibility—but the walls are cracking. With more nations investing in women's teams, the dream of equal cricketing glory is no longer distant.

In classrooms, parks, and slum alleys across the world, little girls now pick up a bat or ball and dream of playing for their country. That's the real victory.

Conclusion: Not the Future—The Present

Women's cricket is not "the future"—it's the **present**. The game is faster, tougher, and more inspiring than ever before. These women didn't just break boundaries—they redrew them.

Because cricket is not about gender. It's about greatness.

Chapter 20: Cricket and Technology – DRS, Hawk-Eye & More

Once upon a time, cricket relied solely on human judgment—an umpire's finger was the final word. No replays, no reviews, no second chances. But as the game evolved and the stakes grew higher, the demand for fairness, accuracy, and drama brought **technology** to the pitch.

Today, cricket is one of the most tech-savvy sports on the planet. From slow-motion replays to predictive ball-tracking, innovations like **DRS**, **Hawk-Eye**, and **Snickometer** have changed how the game is played, watched, and judged.

Let's take a thrilling dive into the world where cricket meets cutting-edge tech.

---

1. The Rise of the Third Umpire

It all began in **1992** during a Test match between South Africa and India. For the first time, the TV umpire—aka the **third umpire**—was used to adjudicate a run-out decision. Since then, there's been no turning back.

With multiple camera angles and high-definition footage, the third umpire now decides on catches, boundaries, no-balls, and more—often under pressure from millions of eyes watching live.

2. DRS – Decision Review System

Launched in **2008**, the **Decision Review System (DRS)** brought revolution. It allowed players to **challenge** on-field umpire decisions—just like a courtroom appeal!

Here's how it works:

- Players signal a review using a "T" sign.
- The third umpire checks multiple technologies: **UltraEdge**, **Hawk-Eye**, and **ball-tracking**.
- The decision is either **UPHELD** or **OVERTURNED**.

This system added a whole new layer of suspense and strategy. A well-timed review can turn a game around. A poor one can waste a golden opportunity.

3. Hawk-Eye – Predicting the Unpredictable

Ever wondered where the ball would have gone if it hadn't hit the pad? **Hawk-Eye** answers that.

Using **six to seven high-speed cameras**, Hawk-Eye tracks the ball's path in real-time and predicts whether it would hit the stumps. It's the magic behind **LBW decisions** and one of the most trusted tools in cricket today.

But it's not always black and white. That's where **"Umpire's Call"** comes in—a grey area that sparks endless debates in living rooms and commentary boxes alike.

4. Snickometer & UltraEdge – Hearing the Unseen

A ball brushing the edge of the bat can be game-changing—but what if the umpire misses it? Enter **Snickometer** and **UltraEdge**.

These tools use **sound waves and graphical spikes** to detect even the faintest of edges. One little spike on the screen can send the batter walking back to the pavilion.

No need for sleuthing anymore—technology catches what the naked eye (and ear) can't.

---

5. Hot Spot – The Heat Signature Truth

Used especially in televised matches, **Hot Spot** uses **infrared cameras** to detect friction. When the ball hits the bat, pad, or glove, a white mark (a hot spot) appears on the screen.

It's like a thermal detective, capturing the hidden evidence of contact.

---

6. SpiderCam, Stump Mic & LED Bails – The Extras That Shine

Technology isn't just for decisions—it enhances the **spectator experience** too.

- **SpiderCam** zooms and glides across the field, giving cinematic views.
- **Stump microphones** catch every sound—from bat thuds to player banter.
- **LED bails** light up instantly when dislodged, helping judge close run-outs with flair.

These features make cricket not just a sport—but a **high-tech spectacle**.

---

7. Future Tech: What's Next?

AI-generated match predictions? Real-time player health analytics? Smart wearables for bowlers and fielders? The possibilities are endless.

Cricket is embracing the digital age with open arms, blending its rich heritage with futuristic innovation.

Conclusion: When Tradition Meets Technology

Purists may argue that too much tech steals the soul of the game. But in reality, technology hasn't replaced tradition—it's **protected it**. It ensures **fair play**, reduces errors, and brings fans closer to the action than ever before.

In the end, cricket is still about bat versus ball, heart versus mind. Technology just makes sure the truth isn't lost in the noise.

Chapter 21: Cricketing Nicknames & Their Backstories

Cricket isn't just about stats and scores—it's full of personality, flair, and stories. One of the quirkiest and most entertaining parts of the game? **Nicknames!**

From "The Little Master" to "Mr. 360," nicknames in cricket aren't just cool titles—they're badges of honor, earned through breathtaking performances, unique styles, or unforgettable moments. These names often stick forever, making players legends both on and off the field.

So, let's dive into some of the most iconic cricketing nicknames and the fascinating stories behind them.

1. Sachin Tendulkar – *The Little Master / Master Blaster*

The name "Little Master" was first associated with Sunil Gavaskar, but when Sachin Tendulkar arrived on the scene—short in stature but mighty with the bat—the title passed on.
 He also earned the nickname **"Master Blaster"** for his explosive batting that dominated bowlers worldwide. In India, he's more than a cricketer—he's a **demi-god**, and his nicknames reflect that legacy.

---

2. AB de Villiers – *Mr. 360*

Why "Mr. 360"? Because AB de Villiers could hit the ball **in any direction**, at any time, with pure genius. Whether it was a reverse sweep over third man or a scoop over fine leg, AB played shots never seen before—and from every angle.
 This nickname celebrates his creativity, athleticism, and unpredictability.

---

3. Muttiah Muralitharan – *Murali the Magician*

With over **800 Test wickets**, Muralitharan spun web after web of destruction. His mysterious arm action and seemingly supernatural turn earned him the magical nickname.
 Facing him was like solving a riddle—with every delivery adding a new twist (literally).

---

4. Glenn McGrath – *Pigeon*

You'd think one of the deadliest fast bowlers would have a fierce nickname, right? But McGrath's lanky frame and thin legs led to teammates teasingly calling him "Pigeon."
 The name stuck—ironically—for a bowler who knocked out batsmen like dominoes.

5. Chris Gayle – *Universe Boss*

Gayle didn't settle for local fame. He called himself the **"Universe Boss"**, and honestly, he backed it up with towering sixes and swag on and off the field.
 This nickname reflects not just power but **attitude, confidence**, and showmanship.

6. Mahendra Singh Dhoni – *Captain Cool*

When others panicked, Dhoni stayed ice-cold. His calm decisions, poker-face expressions, and last-over finishes made him the ultimate **Captain Cool**.
 The name perfectly fits the man who led India to all major ICC trophies with nerves of steel.

7. Shahid Afridi – *Boom Boom Afridi*

The nickname "Boom Boom" came from his aggressive, six-hitting style. Afridi once smashed a 37-ball century in his second ODI match—and fans were hooked for life.
 Every time he walked in, the crowd expected fireworks—and he often delivered.

8. Ricky Ponting – *Punter*

"Punter" came from Ponting's early days when he loved placing bets on greyhound races. It became a dressing room name that followed him into legendhood.
 As a captain, he led Australia through a golden era, but the nickname always brought fans back to his humble, playful beginnings.

9. Lasith Malinga – *Slinga Malinga*

Malinga's nickname came naturally from his **sling-arm action**. It was unorthodox, deceptive, and dangerous.
"Slinga Malinga" was the nightmare of many batsmen, especially at the death overs with those toe-crushing yorkers.

10. Rahul Dravid – *The Wall*

You could build a fortress behind Dravid. Solid, dependable, and immovable, he earned "The Wall" for his incredible defensive technique and concentration.
He once batted for over **12 hours** in a Test innings. That's not just a wall—that's **a fortress of willpower**.

11. Steve Smith – *Smudge*

It may not sound majestic, but "Smudge" is a common Australian nickname for Smiths. What makes it fun is how "Smudge" went from a leg-spinner to the **number one Test batsman**, rewriting batting books with his weird-but-effective technique.

12. Virat Kohli – *King Kohli*

Kohli's aggression, passion, and relentless consistency have crowned him **King Kohli** in the eyes of fans.
He rules the chase like no other and wears his emotions on his sleeve—commanding respect and fear in equal measure.

13. Jacques Kallis – *The Silent Warrior*

Not all legends are loud. Kallis let his bat and ball do the talking. One of the greatest all-rounders in history, his quiet demeanor earned him this nickname—a tribute to his **humility and dominance**.

14. Ravindra Jadeja – *Sir Jadeja*

What started as a meme became a title! "Sir Jadeja" was first a sarcastic joke online, but Jadeja's performances turned it into a badge of honor. Now, he embraces it with a wink—and fans love it.

15. Shoaib Akhtar – *Rawalpindi Express*

The fastest bowler in history wasn't just quick—he was **terrifying**. Born in Rawalpindi, Akhtar's nickname reflects his pace and power—like a train with no brakes.

Why Nicknames Matter

Nicknames in cricket connect fans with players in a personal, emotional way. They reflect **traits, journeys, moments**, and **memories**—often sticking longer than stats.

Whether they're funny, fierce, or heartfelt, these nicknames are part of the sport's soul.

Chapter 22: Fastest Balls, Longest Sixes & Other Extremes

Cricket is often called a gentleman's game—but sometimes, it's also a game of **wild extremes**. Speed that stuns. Sixes that disappear into the sky. Records so outrageous, they sound almost unreal.

This chapter is your **all-access pass to the wildest, fastest, biggest, and most jaw-dropping moments** in cricket history. Buckle up—this is not your average scoreboard.

Fastest Deliveries Ever Bowled

Speed. Terror. Adrenaline.
The fastest bowlers in cricket don't just deliver balls—they launch rockets. Here are the most spine-chilling missiles ever hurled down a pitch:

- **Shoaib Akhtar (Pakistan) – 161.3 km/h (100.23 mph)**
  Bowled against England in the 2003 World Cup, this delivery remains the **fastest ever recorded in cricket**. Nicknamed the "Rawalpindi Express," Akhtar made batsmen flinch before the ball even pitched.

- **Shaun Tait (Australia) – 161.1 km/h**
  Known for his unpredictable and explosive pace, Tait came terrifyingly close to Akhtar's record during an ODI in 2010.

- **Brett Lee (Australia) – 161.1 km/h**
  Smooth run-up, lethal speed. Brett Lee's 2005 delivery against New Zealand was pure poetry in motion—and panic for the batter.

- **Jeff Thomson (Australia) – ~160 km/h (Unofficial)**
  Back in the 1970s, Thomson was the **original speed demon**, with deliveries clocked by primitive radar tech. Imagine his speed with today's tools!

Longest Sixes Ever Hit

When a batter connects just right, the ball doesn't just go over the rope—it vanishes into the stratosphere. Here are some of the **monster hits** that left the earth's atmosphere (almost):

- **Shahid Afridi – 158 meters (vs. South Africa, 2013)**
  Yes, you read that right. This mythical six was sent flying over the stadium roof. Whether it was truly 158m is debated, but fans worldwide still believe in this epic launch.

- **Brett Lee – 130 meters (vs. West Indies)**
  Wait—a fast bowler on the list? That's right. Lee smashed one so far it reportedly landed outside the Gabba!

- **Martin Guptill – 127 meters (vs. South Africa)**
  The calm Kiwi surprised everyone with this jaw-dropping shot in 2012.

- **Chris Gayle – 120+ meters (Multiple times)**
  The **Universe Boss** doesn't just hit sixes—he drops nukes. He's hit **1000+ sixes** in professional cricket, with many clearing well over 100 meters.

Most Sixes in an Inning (Team & Individual)

- **Team Record – 22 Sixes (England vs. Netherlands, 2023 World Cup)**
  The English team treated Dutch bowlers like target practice in Pune.

- **Individual Record – Eoin Morgan (17 sixes vs. Afghanistan, 2019)**
  Morgan wasn't just captain—he was a **one-man airstrike**, breaking records and Afghan hearts in Manchester.

Fastest Century in Any Format

- **AB de Villiers – 31-ball century (ODI vs. West Indies, 2015)**
  This was **batting from another dimension**. AB mixed power, elegance, and 360-degree madness to reach 100 in just 31 balls—still the fastest in ODIs.

- **David Miller – 35 balls (T20I, vs. Bangladesh, 2017)**
  Miller smashed this record with brutal power—earning his nickname "Killer Miller."

- **Chris Gayle – 30-ball century (IPL 2013)**
  In franchise cricket, Gayle lit up Bangalore with the fastest T20 hundred ever—ending with **175 not out**. Unreal.

Other Mind-Blowing Extremes

- **Most Runs in a Single Over – 36 Runs**
  Yuvraj Singh vs. Stuart Broad (T20 World Cup 2007) – Six sixes in six balls. Iconic. Emotional. Historic.
  Also achieved by Herschelle Gibbs (ODI) and Kieron Pollard (T20I).

- **Most Wickets in a Match – Jim Laker (19 wickets in a Test, 1956)**
  Laker turned a Test match into a solo performance, almost single-handedly bowling out Australia.

- **Longest Test Innings – Hanif Mohammad (970 minutes / 337 runs)**
  That's **over 16 hours** at the crease! True grit.

- **Highest Individual Score in ODIs – Rohit Sharma (264 runs)**
  That's more than an entire team sometimes manages!

Why We Love the Extremes

These aren't just numbers—they're **moments that shook the cricketing universe**. They're the reason fans gasp, cheer, cry, and remember.

Because when cricket hits the extreme, it becomes unforgettable.

Chapter 23: Rare Feats – Hat-tricks, Double Centuries & More

Cricket is a game of strategy, skill, and sometimes... sheer magic. Among the thousands of matches played across formats, there are moments so rare, so exceptional, that they make fans sit up, gasp, and remember where they were when it happened. These are the feats that **don't just win games—they become legends**.

Let's dive into the **world of cricket's rarest milestones**—from hat-tricks that shocked the world to double centuries that redefined possibility.

Hat-Tricks: Three Balls, Three Wickets, One Roar

Taking a wicket is tough. Taking three in three consecutive balls? That's cricketing wizardry.

- **Wasim Akram (Pakistan)** – One of the few to take *two Test hat-tricks* in his career. When the "Sultan of Swing" was on fire, even the best batsmen were helpless.

- **Lasith Malinga (Sri Lanka)** – The **king of death bowling** once took *four wickets in four balls*—a feat so rare, it looked scripted.

- **Chetan Sharma (India)** – The **first bowler to claim a World Cup hat-trick**, back in 1987. A proud moment for Indian cricket.

- **Brett Lee, Kemar Roach, and Saqlain Mushtaq** – Each etched their names in World Cup history with thrilling hat-tricks that flipped matches upside down.

Hat-tricks aren't just statistics—they're explosions of adrenaline. They can turn quiet stadiums into thunderous arenas in a matter of minutes.

Double Centuries in ODIs: A Once Unthinkable Feat

There was a time when a **century in ODIs** was a big deal. Then came the double tons—**a cricketing revolution**.

- **Sachin Tendulkar (India)** – The **first-ever man** to score a double century in ODIs. His 200* against South Africa in 2010 broke the barrier and opened the floodgates.

- **Rohit Sharma (India)** – Not once, not twice, but **three times**! Including the highest ever—**264 runs** against Sri Lanka. A masterclass in timing, power, and patience.

- **Virender Sehwag, Martin Guptill, Chris Gayle, Fakhar Zaman** – Each joined the elite club with their own brand of destruction.

What was once thought impossible is now a badge of elite batting greatness.

Test Triple Centuries: The Everest of Patience

Scoring 300 runs in a single Test inning isn't just rare—it's mentally and physically **grueling**.

- **Brian Lara (West Indies)** – Holds the record for the **highest individual score in Test cricket – 400 not out!** He also scored 375 earlier. Lara didn't break records—he rewrote them.

- **Virender Sehwag (India)** – Fearless and destructive, he smashed two triple centuries, including a 319 against South Africa.

- **Chris Gayle, Karun Nair, Sanath Jayasuriya** – Each made it into the elite triple-ton club with powerful and unforgettable performances.

T20I Centuries: Lightning Strikes

In a format where batters usually have just 20 overs to shine, scoring a century is **blazing brilliance**.

- **Suryakumar Yadav, Glenn Maxwell, Babar Azam** – These players have shown how to build masterpieces in lightning speed.

- **Aaron Finch – 172 vs Zimbabwe** – The highest score in T20 Internationals ever. A complete demolition job.

A T20I century isn't just rare—it's a controlled explosion.

All-Round Feats: The Golden Double

Some performances are *so complete*, they feel like the work of two players in one:

- **Shakib Al Hasan (Bangladesh)** – Scored 600+ runs and took 10 wickets in the **2019 World Cup**. A statistical miracle.

- **Kapil Dev, Jacques Kallis, Ben Stokes** – These legends won games with both bat and ball—true all-round giants.

The Rarest of the Rare

- **Six Sixes in an Over** – Only a handful have done it: *Yuvraj Singh, Herschelle Gibbs, Kieron Pollard*.

- **Hat-trick on Debut** – Few bowlers have taken a hat-trick in their first-ever match. *Narendra Hirwani, Damien Fleming,* and *Taijul Islam* are among them.

- **Century & 10 Wickets in a Test** – Only **Ian Botham** and **Shakib Al Hasan** have done this. Insane domination.

Why Rare Feats Matter

They remind us why we watch cricket. They **shock us, delight us, and give us goosebumps**. These aren't everyday highlights—they're **once-in-a-lifetime cricketing gems** that live forever in history.

Chapter 24: Cricket & Pop Culture – Movies, Songs & References

Cricket isn't just a sport—it's a global **obsession that spills over into movies, music, fashion, and daily conversation**. From Bollywood blockbusters to Hollywood documentaries, from stadium anthems to memes that break the internet, cricket is everywhere. It's the thread that connects generations, regions, and even those who've never held a bat.

Let's dive into how cricket has become an unforgettable part of pop culture across the world.

Bollywood & Cricket: A Love Affair

In India, **cricket and cinema are the twin religions**, and when they collide, magic happens.

- **"Lagaan" (2001)** – Perhaps the most iconic cricket movie of all time, this Oscar-nominated film blended colonial tension, village pride, and a nail-biting cricket match into a cinematic masterpiece.

- **"MS Dhoni: The Untold Story" (2016)** – A biopic that captured the rise of one of India's greatest captains. It wasn't just a film—it was a celebration.

- **"83" (2021)** – This film brought India's first Cricket World Cup victory to life, with Ranveer Singh embodying the legendary Kapil Dev. Goosebumps guaranteed.

- **"Iqbal"**, **"Jersey"**, and **"Kai Po Che!"** – Each of these movies showed cricket as more than a sport—it was a symbol of **dreams, struggle, and triumph**.

Hollywood & Global Documentaries

While Bollywood dramatizes cricket beautifully, **Hollywood and global platforms** have captured the sport's reality and emotional depth:

- **"Fire in Babylon"** – A brilliant documentary that shows how the West Indies team of the 1970s and 80s **used cricket as resistance and pride** against racism and colonialism.

- **"The Test" (Amazon Prime)** – A behind-the-scenes look at the Australian team post the infamous ball-tampering scandal, showing resilience and rebuilding.

- **"Roar of the Lion"** – A docu-series about MS Dhoni and the Chennai Super Kings, blending IPL craze with personal redemption.

These films and series have taken cricket **beyond the field** and shown fans the human stories behind the headlines.

Cricket in Music: Stadium Anthems & Street Beats

Whether it's the thumping beat of a World Cup anthem or a catchy jingle that plays on every cricket broadcast, **music and cricket go hand in hand**.

- **"Chak De India"**, **"Kar Har Maidan Fateh"**, and **"Vande Mataram"** – Songs that have become cricket anthems in India.

- **"Stand Up For The Champions"** – Often played during trophy presentations, this global track is etched into cricket fans' memories.

- **IPL Theme Songs** – Whether it's "India ka Tyohaar" or regional team jingles, the music fuels the **festival vibe of cricket**.

In street cricket matches across the subcontinent, Bluetooth speakers blast energetic tunes that make even gully matches feel like World Cups.

Fashion & Catchphrases: From Jerseys to Memes

Cricket stars are now **style icons and trendsetters**.

- **Virat Kohli's beard**, **Dhoni's cool demeanor**, **Rohit Sharma's shades**, or **Hardik Pandya's bling**—fans don't just watch them; they copy them.

- Team jerseys have become **everyday wear**, from kids on the streets to fans at weddings (yes, it happens!).

- And let's not forget the **catchphrases**:
    - "Howzzat!"
    - "Dhoni finishes off in style!"
    - "Boom Boom Afridi!"
    - "Gabbar is back!" (Shikhar Dhawan style)

These lines have entered everyday conversations, social media captions, and even political speeches.

Memes, Ads & Social Media Craze

Cricket has taken over **Instagram reels, Twitter battles, and viral memes**.

- A dropped catch? Expect memes in minutes.
- A funny reaction from Kohli or Stokes? It's a sticker on WhatsApp by nightfall.

Ads like **"Mauka Mauka"** during World Cups became iconic, generating laughs, debates, and millions of views.

Why It Matters

Cricket's presence in pop culture isn't accidental—it's the result of the sport's **emotional power, dramatic highs and lows, and deep-rooted connection with people's identities**.

It doesn't matter whether you're in Mumbai or Melbourne—**cricket is no longer just about runs and wickets**. It's about cinema, soundtracks, slang, and swag. It's a lifestyle.

Conclusion: Why the World Loves Cricket

Cricket is more than just a sport. It's a **global heartbeat**, a drama played out on green fields under the sun and lights, where emotions run high, heroes are born, and history is written with every bat swing and ball bowled.

From the narrow gullies of Mumbai to the quiet parks of London, from the dusty grounds of Karachi to the vibrant stadiums of Melbourne—**cricket unites people** across languages, cultures, and continents. It doesn't matter if you're a die-hard fan or a casual watcher, cricket has a magical way of **pulling you in, ball by ball**.

So why does the world love cricket?

1. The Drama of Uncertainty

No other sport captures the **thrill of unpredictability** like cricket. A team needing 100 runs with just 5 balls left? We've seen it happen. A hat-trick in the final over? Been there. The tension, the nail-biting finishes, the dramatic twists—**it's a real-life thriller every time**.

2. The Characters

From legends like **Sachin Tendulkar, Sir Don Bradman, and Muttiah Muralitharan** to modern icons like **Virat Kohli, Babar Azam, Ben Stokes, and Ellyse Perry**, cricket has always been rich with **personalities that inspire, entertain, and provoke**. These players become household names, role models, and sometimes even national symbols.

3. The Stories

Behind every cricketer is a story—of struggle, sacrifice, and success. Teams like **Afghanistan**, who rose from conflict zones, or **West Indies**, who ruled the world with flair, or **Ireland and Netherlands**, who shocked giants—cricket is full of **underdog tales and legendary journeys** that stay in your heart.

4. The Passion

Cricket fans are unlike any other. They **paint their faces, chant for hours, cry after losses**, and dance in the streets after wins. The emotion, the dedication, the love—it's something you feel in every stadium, pub, or living room where the game is watched.

5. The Culture

Cricket isn't limited to boundaries—it's woven into **music, films, fashion, and even politics**. Whether it's a World Cup anthem, a cricket-themed movie, or a political leader quoting a cricketing term, the sport is part of our cultural DNA.

6. The Global Community

Whether it's a West Indies fan vibing with an Indian supporter, or a Pakistani and Australian discussing Test cricket over Twitter—**cricket brings people together**. It sparks debates, builds friendships, and creates a global family that speaks one common language: **cricket**.

In the end, the world loves cricket because cricket loves the world back. It gives us moments of joy, unity, heartbreak, and glory. It teaches patience, courage, respect, and resilience.

Cricket is not just a game.
It's a **passion, a memory, a celebration**.
And most of all—it's a way of life.

Long live cricket.

Closing Note: From One Cricket Lover to Another

Dear Reader,

If you've reached this page, I know one thing for sure—**cricket lives inside you**, just like it lives inside me.

This book wasn't written just with facts and stats. It was written with **childhood memories of Sunday matches**, the thrill of staying up late for overseas tours, the heartbreaks of close defeats, and the goosebumps of iconic victories.

It was written with the **sound of leather on willow echoing in my ears**, the roar of the crowd in my heart, and the names of legends whispering through every chapter.

Maybe you remembered your first six, or the time you argued passionately with friends over who's the real GOAT. Maybe you smiled thinking about Dhoni's calm face, Gayle's swagger, Malinga's sling, or Ellyse Perry's grace.
 And maybe, just maybe, this book reminded you why **cricket is not just a sport—it's a feeling**.

I didn't write this book *for* you.
I wrote it **with you**.

With every cricket fan who has ever shouted at a screen, worn a lucky jersey, or prayed before the final over.

So, thank you for being part of this journey.

And remember—whenever life gets tough, find a quiet corner, close your eyes, and replay that moment when your favorite player hit a six, took a blinder, or lifted the trophy.

Because in those moments, **we don't just watch cricket—we live it**.

With all my love,
– A Fellow Cricket Fan

Printed in Dunstable, United Kingdom